*Arise, shine, for your light has come, and the glory of the Lord rises upon you.
See, darkness covers the earth, and thick darkness is over the peoples,
but the Lord rises upon you and His glory appears over you.
Nations will come to your light, and kings to the brightness of your dawn*
(Isaiah 60:1-3).

But you, O mountains of Israel, will produce branches and fruit for My people Israel, for they will soon come home (Ezekiel 36:8).

Judea & Samaria
The Biblical Heartland of Israel

REV. HENK POOT AND THEO HORNEMAN

Copyright © 2010—Christians for Israel International/Theo Horneman
Photographs and graphic design—© 2010 Theo Horneman

All rights reserved. This book is protected under the copyright laws. This book may not be copied or reprinted for commercial gain or profit. The use of short quotations or occasional page copying for personal or group study is permitted and encouraged. Permission will be granted upon request. Unless otherwise identified, Scripture quotations are taken from the Holy Bible, New International Version®, Copyright © 1973, 1978, 1984 International Bible Society. Used by permission of Zondervan. All rights reserved. Scripture quotations marked KJV are taken from the King James Version. Scripture quotations marked NASB are taken from the New American Standard Bible®, Copyright © 1960, 1962, 1963, 1968, 1971, 1972, 1973, 1975, 1977, 1995 by The Lockman Foundation. Used by permission.

Concept by Henk Poot and Theo Horneman
Text by Henk Poot
Photographs by Theo Horneman
Pictured on cover: Michal Hallel – Kfar Tapuach, Samaria

DESTINY IMAGE™ EUROPE srl
Via Maiella, 1
66020 San Giovanni Teatino (Ch) — Italy

"Changing the world, one book at a time."

This book and all other Destiny Image™ Europe books are available at Christian bookstores and distributors worldwide.

To order products, or for any other correspondence:

DESTINY IMAGE™ EUROPE srl
Via della Scafa 29/14
65013 Città Sant'Angelo (Pe) — Italy
Tel. +39 085 4716623 • +39 085 8670146
Email: info@eurodestinyimage.com
Or reach us on the Internet: www.eurodestinyimage.com

ISBN: 978-88-96727-18-8

For Worldwide Distribution, Printed in Israel.
1 2 3 4 5 6 7 8 / 14 13 12 11 11

Proceeds from the sale of this book will be used to support the people of Judea and Samaria.
For more information see www.judeaandsamaria.com

Dedication

We dedicate this book to the pioneers of Judea and Samaria.

You are bringing the heartland of Israel back to life.

Together, we believe that God is fulfilling His promises to the Jewish people.

Together, we look for the coming of Messiah.

May that day come soon.

Acknowledgments

We wish to thank Christians for Israel and Christian Friends of Israeli Communities (CFOIC Heartland) for making this book possible.

Special thanks to Sondra Oster Baras (CFOIC Heartland) for providing on-site assistance and editing.

Thank you to the team at Destiny Image Europe for believing in this project.

Above all, we want to thank all our friends in Judea and Samaria for being faithful to God's Word and for letting us share your hopes and dreams.

Henk Poot and *Theo Horneman*

Forewords

The biblical lands of Judea and Samaria are generally referred to as the West Bank, or the "occupied territories." But can Israel be an occupying power in its own land? In Psalm 105:7-11 we read: "He is the Lord our God; His judgments are in all the earth. He remembers His covenant forever, the word He commanded, for a thousand generations, the covenant He made with Abraham, the oath He swore to Isaac. He confirmed it to Jacob as a decree, to Israel as an everlasting covenant: 'To you I will give the land of Canaan as the portion you will inherit.'" According to the Bible, Israel does not exist by the grace of the United Nations, but by the grace of God on the basis of an everlasting covenant to which the Lord swore a solemn oath. According to the Bible, the Lord cannot lie nor break an oath; therefore, He will be true to His everlasting covenant with Israel.

Israel's right to possess the whole of the Promised Land—including parts of today's Jordan and Syria, the "East Bank"—is firmly grounded in the Bible, even without relying on the expanded borders during the reigns of King David and King Solomon. The boundaries of the Promised Land under Joshua, after the Exodus from Egypt, included the Golan (biblical Bashan), Judea and Samaria (the West Bank), and part of the East Bank.

It is remarkable that Israel accepted the United Nations' Partition Plan of 1947 when the Arab nations rejected it. Throughout history, European countries have initiated colonial wars that enlarged their territories. Israel, by contrast, has only been involved in defensive wars. Since the establishment of the State of Israel, the neighboring Arab nations launched many wars with the express purpose of annihilating the Jewish state and driving the Jews into the sea; miraculously, these wars actually led to the expansion of Israeli territory. And yet, the western media and others insist on referring to Jewish pioneers in underdeveloped areas as "settlers," a pejorative term which is biased against Israel and supports the one-sided pro-Palestinian and pro-Arab approach to developments in the Middle East.

This book offers a glimpse of many places in the heart of the Promised Land. They are all located in the biblical lands of Judea and Samaria. Israel's holiest cities are located here.

Open this beautiful book of photographs and visit these Biblical sites:

Hebron was a very important city for Israel. It is located 35 kilometers south of Jerusalem and is blessed with vineyards and orchards. The city was given to Caleb, who, together with Joshua, returned a positive report about the Promised Land (see Josh. 14:6-15; Num. 13). Sarah died in Hebron—also referred to as Kiryat Arba—and she is buried there (see Gen. 23:2,19). Isaac died in Hebron as well (see Gen. 35:27-29). Abraham, Isaac, and Jacob are buried in Hebron, as are Sarah, Rebecca, and Leah—in the cave in the field of Machpelah, near Mamre, which Abraham bought as a burial place from Ephron the Hittite, along with the field (see Gen. 49:29-33; 50:12-14). The patriarchs and matriarchs of Israel are buried in Hebron. And we worship the God of Abraham, Isaac, and Jacob. For centuries, there was a large Jewish population in Hebron, but in 1929 Arabs massacred many Jews and they were evacuated by the British. In 1936, after another attempt to settle in Hebron, the Jews fled from their Arab attackers. But today, Jews are living in Hebron once again and in the neighboring town of Kiryat Arba, even though they are often ferociously attacked.

The city of Shechem is located between Mount Ebal and Mount Gerizim. Abraham built an altar here (see Gen. 12:6-7). Jacob pitched his tent here, bought a piece of land, and built an altar to the Lord (see Gen. 33:18-20). Later, Joseph was buried here (see Josh. 24:32). Under Joshua's leadership, the children of Israel renewed their covenant with the Lord, the God of Israel (see Josh. 24:1-27). In recent years, we have witnessed the total desecration of Joseph's tomb by Islamic Arab nationalists. They set fire to the building, a Jewish shrine, and then repaired it and converted it into a mosque.

At Shiloh, Joshua erected the Tabernacle and cast lots to apportion the land among the tribes of Israel in the presence of the Lord (see Josh. 18:1-10; 19:51). During the time of the Judges, the House of God was in Shiloh, the first place that He established a dwelling for His Name (see Judg. 18:31; 1 Sam. 1:3; Jer. 7:12). It was in Shiloh that Hannah received the promise that she would have a son named Samuel, and she dedicated him to the House of the Lord (see 1 Sam. 1).

There are many other places in Samaria and Judea that you will see in this book, like Bethel, Bethlehem, Samaria, and Gibeon, all located in the areas that are referred to today as the "occupied territories." This is the land of the Bible. This is the land of the kings of Israel and Judah. The land of the prophets of Israel. This is the land from "Dan to Beersheba." (See Judges 20:1; 1 Samuel 3:20; 2 Samuel 3:10; 17:11; 24:2,15; 1 Kings 4:25; 1 Chronicles 21:2; 2 Chronicles 30:5.) The land that Abraham walked from north to south, from east to west (see Gen. 13:14-17). This is the land that was promised to Abraham and to Israel in an everlasting Covenant made by the eternal God.

Rev. Henk Poot and photographer Theo Horneman have created an impressive book indeed, focusing on areas that are as much a part of Israel as those areas within the so-called "Green Line," at least from a biblical perspective.

Rev. Willem J.J. Glashouwer
President, Christians for Israel International

When the Dutch edition of this book was released, I showed it to friends of mine who had once lived in Gush Katif, the Jewish areas of Gaza which were destroyed in the summer of 2005. Together, we were members of the settlement movement which initiated the development of close to 200 Jewish communities throughout Judea, Samaria, and Gaza. When these former residents of Gush Katif saw the title of the book—*Judea and Samaria*—they looked at me in a mixture of surprise and pain. "What happened to us?" they asked. But we both knew the answer—their communities, created from the same biblical motivation as the communities in Judea and Samaria, had been destroyed.

Most of the world saw the reality of life in the Gaza communities during the hours of their destruction. For the first time, they were introduced to towns and villages that included beautiful homes and gardens, farms, schools, and shopping and cultural centers. But by the time people understood what had existed in Gaza, it had all been bulldozed to rubble.

The future of Judea and Samaria is periodically put on the negotiating table as the international community has become used to dealing with this area as "occupied territory"—an area foreign to Israel's existence and not really belonging to the Jewish people. Nothing could be further from the truth. Judea and Samaria represent the very heartland of biblical Israel, the cradle of Jewish civilization, the mountains and valleys which witnessed the birth of the Jewish nation.

This book tells that story in pictures, with accompanying Scriptures and brief explanations. This book gives the nations of the world the opportunity to see for themselves what Judea and Samaria have become—an area of Jewish villages and towns, the rebirth of a Jewish presence in an area that is rich in Jewish history.

I am a "settler" myself, and as the director of the Israel office of CFOIC Heartland for more than ten years, I have linked Christians from all over the world with the Jewish communities in Judea and Samaria. Through my work, I have met so many wonderful people who have pledged their support for the people of these communities in their struggle to hold onto their land.

We cannot afford another Disengagement. We cannot afford the destruction of any more Jewish communities. As you turn the pages of this book, as you learn of the communities and gain a better understanding of their scriptural context, I hope you will pledge to support these people as well. Let's work together to ensure that people all over the world understand the reality of biblical Israel before it is too late.

Sondra Oster Baras
Director, Israel Office
CFOIC Heartland

Introduction

This book is about the tribal areas of Judah, Ephraim, Manasseh, and Benjamin.

This is where biblical places like Hebron are located, where Abraham buried his wife Sarah, and where David became King over Judah. This is where Bethel is located, where Jacob dreamt his dream of the ladder to Heaven, and where God confirmed His promises to him. This is where Shiloh is located, where the tabernacle stood for centuries.

This is the area of Shechem and Ai, Tekoa, Mt. Abel, Mechola, Gilgal. This is the land of Elon Moreh where Abraham pitched his first tent in the Land of Canaan and where the Lord showed him the land that He had designated for all eternity as the land of a nation that would yet be born—the nation of Israel.

This book is about Samaria and Judea, the heritage of two spies, Joshua and Caleb, who believed that the promises of the Lord would be fulfilled regardless of political favor or the permission of nations.

This book is about the heartland of Israel, a highly strategic area. These are the mountains of Israel, and whoever inhabits these mountains controls the coastal plain below, including Tel Aviv and the important access routes to Jerusalem. But the heartland of Israel is also a prophetic region. For the Messiah will return upon the Mount of Olives and will feed His flock on the mountains of Israel!

Perhaps this is the true reason why Israel's claim to Samaria and Judea is so controversial today. To the nations of the world, these areas have been stripped of their biblical identity and are known as "the occupied territories" or simply the "West Bank," and on many maps this region has been separated from the rest of Israel and is called Palestine.

This book will introduce you to the 280,000 Jews who live in Judea and Samaria. Who are these people and what does their life look like? Theo and I have chosen to focus on the smaller villages. We have not emphasized the major cities of Ariel, with its own university, or Maale Adumim, the major suburb of Jerusalem in the direction of Jericho. While these places are important, indeed, their very existence is not under discussion in the current diplomatic arena. We have not focused on Jerusalem either, as that city is already well-known to readers.

Samaria and Judea were occupied by the Jordanian Army in 1948 during Israel's War of Independence, and this occupation lasted until 1967. During this period, almost nothing was done by the Jordanians to develop the area, and large parts were only accessible to the military. There were Arabs living there, but many Arabs arrived in the area only after the Jews returned. (For example, approximately 400,000 people from Syria, Jordan, and Northern Africa entered the area between 1976 and 2000. They entered Israel initially on tourist visas but many stayed because of better social and economic conditions than their home country.)

In 1967, Israel was attacked on all sides by Syria, Jordan, and Egypt. Their armies marched against Israel in order to destroy her, but Israel was victorious. In just six days, the biblical areas of Israel's heartland were reunited with the rest of Israel. In 1967, the Jews returned to the villages of Gush Etzion on Jerusalem's southern entrance, which had been destroyed by the Arab Legion in 1948. In 1968 the Jews returned to Hebron for the first time since the Jewish community was massacred and driven from the city in 1929. Only after the Yom Kippur War of 1973 did the Jewish pioneers head for the desolated areas of Samaria, Benjamin, and the Jordan Valley.

Daniella Weiss, former mayor and founder of Kedumim, tells us her story:

"We were in shock that we were attacked on Yom Kippur, the holiest day of the Jewish year. How did God allow this to happen? But then we understood that Hashem wanted to open our eyes: We had left the land He gave us as it was. We didn't do anything with it. It was in those very days that we began to climb the dark and desolate hills of Samaria. First we lived in tents, then came the caravans and after that we built houses. And the land came back to life again. Nature revived and the birds returned. The land was married again by the sons and daughters of Israel."

The Jews who live in Samaria and Judea do so because they believe that the Lord has returned the children of Israel to the Promised Land and because they believe that the heartland is an indissoluble part of that land. As Jews, they believe that God is fulfilling His promises and that the Messiah is coming. We share that belief and that expectation.

We put together this book in order to open the eyes of people who think that the West Bank has nothing to do with Israel. And we present this book as a note of encouragement to the Jewish residents of Samaria and Judea. They are standing in the long tradition of their patriarchs, of the judges, kings, and prophets of Israel, of Joshua, Caleb, David, and Elijah. They are living in the land in a way that demonstrates to the entire world that the redemption of Israel and of the world is near at hand. And they have brought the heartland of Israel back to life.

Rev. Henk Poot
Christians for Israel

Benjamin
The Biblical Heartland of Israel

Benjamin is the region known in the Bible for the fierce conflict with the Philistines in the first years of the Kingdom of Israel. It is the land where the prophet Samuel set up a stone after the victory of Israel at Mitzpah and called its name Eben'ezer—"hitherto the Lord has helped us."

Anatot	Dolev
Maale Adumim	Talmon
Geva-Binyamin	Kochav Yaacov
Migron	Psagot
Amona	Bethel
Neve Tzuf	

It is here that the atrocity of Gibeah took place that led to the war between Benjamin and the rest of the nation. But the smallest tribal area of the Jewish people is also well-known because Jerusalem, with its Temple of the Lord, is situated in her midst.

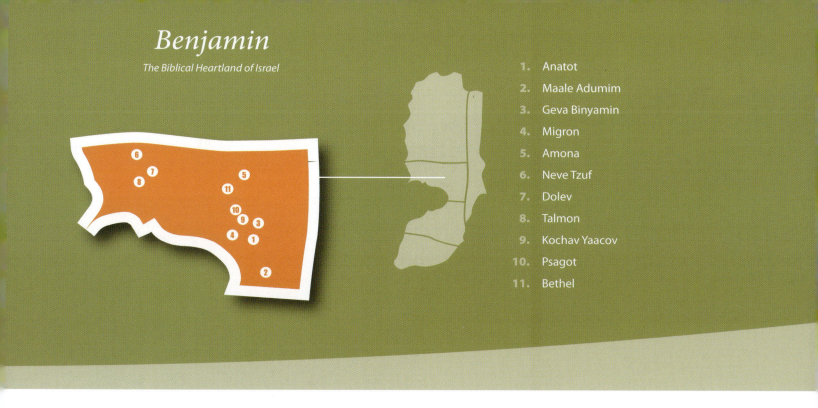

Moses said of Benjamin:

Let the beloved of the Lord rest secure in Him, for He shields him all day long, and the one the Lord loves rests between His shoulders (Deuteronomy 33:12).

Anatot
Benjamin, the Biblical Heartland of Israel

In the Bible, Anatoth is mentioned as one of the Levite cities and as the home of Jeremiah (see Josh. 21:18).

The words of Jeremiah son of Hilkiah, one of the priests at Anathoth in the territory of Benjamin. The word of the Lord came to him in the thirteenth year of the reign of Josiah son of Amon king of Judah (Jeremiah 1:1-2).

When the King of Babylonia besieged Jerusalem, Jeremiah bought a field from his cousin in Anatoth as a token that Israel would once again be restored:

Fields will be bought for silver, and deeds will be signed, sealed and witnessed in the territory of Benjamin, in the villages around Jerusalem, in the towns of Judah and in the towns of the hill country, of the western foothills and of the Negev, because I will restore their fortunes, declares the Lord (Jeremiah 32:44).

The present-day Anatot, also known as Almon, was established in 1982.
It is situated five kilometers north of Jerusalem and is home to 160 families.

I will rejoice in doing them good and will assuredly plant them in this land with all My heart and soul (Jeremiah 32:41).

Maale Adumim
Benjamin, the Biblical Heartland of Israel

Traveling eastward from Jerusalem is Maale Adumim, begun initially as a small community, but today a large city.

Thou hast increased the nation, O Lord, Thou hast increased the nation: Thou art glorified: Thou hadst removed it far unto all the ends of the earth (Isaiah 26:15 KJV).

Geva-Binyamin
Benjamin, the Biblical Heartland of Israel

In the war between Israel and the Philistines, Jonathan occupied Geva. From there, he launched his attack against the Philistine army encamped in Michmas.

The Philistines assembled to fight Israel, with three thousand chariots, six thousand charioteers, and soldiers as numerous as the sand on the seashore. They went up and camped at Michmas, east of Beth Aven (see 1 Sam. 13:5).

Jonathan said to his young armor-bearer, "Come, let's go over to the outpost of those uncircumcised fellows. Perhaps the Lord will act in our behalf. Nothing can hinder the Lord from saving, whether by many or by few." …The men of the outpost shouted to Jonathan and his armor-bearer, "Come up to us and we'll teach you a lesson." So Jonathan said to his armor-bearer, "Climb up after me; the Lord has given them into the hand of Israel." Jonathan climbed up, using his hands and feet, with his armor-bearer right behind him.

The Philistines fell before Jonathan, and his armor-bearer followed and killed behind him. ...Then panic struck the whole army—those in the camp and field, and those in the outposts and raiding parties—and the ground shook. It was a panic sent by God (1 Samuel 14:6,12-13,15).

During this decisive battle, King Saul was on the other side of Michmas, on the hill of Migron, where there was a large water source:

Saul was staying on the outskirts of Gibea under a pomegranate tree in Migron. With him were about six hundred men (1 Samuel 14:2).

When his guards noticed the tumult and confusion in the camp of the enemy, Saul assembled his men and joined the battle. His victory over the Philistines was a great one indeed.

Today Geva-Binyamin is known as Adam. It is situated some three kilometers north of Jerusalem and is well-known for its bakery, where many residents of the surrounding communities buy their challah for Shabbat.

The village numbers 800 families.

Migron
Benjamin, the Biblical Heartland of Israel

Migron, an extension of Kochav Yaakov, is situated on one of the highest hills in this region and is, therefore, of immense strategic importance.

Not far from the Arab village of Michmas lies the Jewish community of Maale Michmas.

Amona
Benjamin, the Biblical Heartland of Israel

Amona was founded in 1997 on a barren hilltop near Ofra. At the end of 2005, there were 30 families living there. When the first permanent houses were built, the government intervened at the insistence of the left-wing organization "Peace Now," which alleged that part of the land belonged to Palestinian Arabs. Despite evidence of forged papers on the Arab side, the nine permanent houses were demolished on February 1, 2006.

Facing a police force of 10,000 men stood 4,000 residents of Judea and Samaria and their supporters. Following later Knesset inquiries, the minister of internal security was held responsible for the unnecessary violence that was used that day against the residents of Amona and their sympathizers.

Amona is mentioned in Joshua 18:24 as Kfar Haämoni.

Though the fig tree should not blossom
And there be no fruit on the vines,
Though the yield of the olive should fail
And the fields produce no food,
Though the flock should be cut off from the fold
And there be no cattle in the stalls,

Yet I will exult in the Lord,
I will rejoice in the God of my salvation.
The Lord God is my strength,
And He has made my feet like hinds' feet,
And makes me walk on my high places
(Habakkuk 3:17-19 NASB).

Neve Tzuf
Benjamin, the Biblical Heartland of Israel

Neve Tzuf was founded on the site of a former British police station from the Mandate period that had been nicknamed "The Fortress," evidence that even during the British period, this hilltop was considered of strategic value.

Perched on a beautiful mountain range at the edge of the coastal plane, this community overlooks the city of Tel Aviv.

After the peace agreement with Egypt in October 1977, the government of Israel decided to develop this region. A month later, the foundation for Neve Tzuf was laid.

Today, there are 225 families living in Neve Tzuf, nearly one thousand people.

There are several schools located in this community, including a "Mechina," where young men receive a religious education before entering the army.

Neve Tzuf has a medical center, a voluntary fire brigade and an Israeli Army post.

In Talmudic times there was a town located on this very spot called Halamish.

Dolev
Benjamin, the Biblical Heartland of Israel

Dolev, established in 1983, is a community of 150 families. Dolev is well-known for its high school for girls with special needs. With the assistance of a psychologist, personal coaches, and social workers, these young girls from all over the country have the opportunity for a new life and receive the education and personal attention they need to succeed.

Although most of the residents of Dolev are "Sabras," the community also includes immigrants from Russia and France.

Then our sons in their youth will be like well-nurtured plants, and our daughters will be like pillars carved to adorn a palace. Our barns will be filled with every kind of provision. Our sheep will increase by thousands, by tens of thousands in our fields; our oxen will draw heavy loads. There will be no breaching of walls, no going into captivity, no cry of distress in our streets. Blessed are the people of whom this is true; blessed are the people whose God is the Lord (Psalm 144:12–15).

Talmon
Benjamin, the Biblical Heartland of Israel

Surrounded on all sides by hostile Arab villages, Talmon is a community that has suffered from the terrorist attacks of recent years. In spite of that, there are 200 families living in Talmon today, including 500 children. The village was founded in 1989 and is named after a family of Temple gatekeepers who helped to rebuild the walls of Jerusalem during the time of Nehemiah.

The Levites in the holy city totaled 284. The gatekeepers: Akkub, Talmon and their associates, who kept watch at the gates—172 men (Nehemiah 11:18-19).

Kochav Yaakov
Benjamin, the Biblical Heartland of Israel

Today, Kochav Yaakov, including the new neighborhood of Tel Zion, numbers more than 1,200 families. There are shops, schools, and a large number of synagogues filled with the many residents who have returned to the Land of Israel from all corners of the earth.

The school in Kochav Yaakov is named after Rabbi Zvi Yehuda Kook, one of the important founders of the Religious Zionist movement.

During the Second Temple period, the area surrounding modern-day Kochav Yaakov was an important agricultural area. The hills were covered with orchards and vines, and the countless remains of winepresses everywhere bear witness to that today.

When you look today at the empty hills of Benjamin that surround Kochav Yaakov, it is hard to imagine how fertile and densely populated this region once was.

You can taste something of the prophecy of Jeremiah who once proclaimed about the land of Israel:

I looked at the earth, and it was formless and empty; and at the heavens, and their light was gone.
I looked at the mountains, and they were quaking; all the hills were swaying.
I looked, and there were no people; every bird in the sky had flown away.
I looked, and the fruitful land was a desert; all its towns lay in ruins before the Lord, before His fierce anger
(Jeremiah 4:23-26).

But today, the Promised Land is coming to life again with the return of the children of Abraham. At the horizon, a golden light is falling upon the new city of Jerusalem, and after centuries the vision of the prophet Joel is becoming a reality:

In that day the mountains will drip new wine, and the hills will flow with milk; all the ravines of Judah will run with water. A fountain will flow out of the Lord's house and will water the valley of acacias (Joel 3:18).

Psagot
Benjamin, the Biblical Heartland of Israel

Literally a stone's throw from Ramallah is the community of Psagot with 1,500 people, including more than 900 children. Psagot is known for its institution where students are educated in Jewish Religious Law.

On the edge of the community facing Ramallah is a concrete wall that has been built to protect community residents, the local elementary school, and the kindergarten against snipers.

At the foot of Psagot lies the biblical Ai, known from the Book of Joshua, but also one of the first places where Abraham settled after arriving in the Promised Land:

From there he went on towards the hills east of Bethel and pitched his tent, with Bethel on the west and Ai on the east. There he built an altar to the Lord and called on the name of the Lord (Genesis 12:8).

Bethel
Benjamin, the Biblical Heartland of Israel

He had a dream in which he saw a stairway resting on the earth, with its top reaching to heaven, and the angels of God were ascending and descending on it. There above it stood the Lord, and He said: "I am the Lord, the God of your father Abraham and the God of Isaac. I will give you and your descendants the land on which you are lying" (Genesis 28:12-13).

When Jacob awoke from his sleep, he thought, "Surely the Lord is in this place, and I was not aware of it." He was afraid and said, "How awesome is this place! This is none other than the house of God (Beth-El); this is the gate of heaven" (Genesis 28:16-17).

Early the next morning Jacob took the stone he had placed under his head and set it up as a pillar and poured oil on top of it. He called that place Bethel… (Genesis 28:18-19).

After the split between Israel and Judah, Jeroboam, the first ruler of the Kingdom of the Ten Tribes, built a sanctuary in Bethel. In this manner he tried to prevent his people from visiting the Temple in Jerusalem (1 Kings 12:28). He made two calves of gold; he set one in Bethel, and he declared to the people that this was the god of Israel. Years later, the prophet Hosea fiercely denounces the sin of Jeroboam:

They are from Israel! This calf—a craftsman has made it; it is not God. It will be broken in pieces, that calf of Samaria (Hosea 8:6).

The prophetess Deborah judged Israel near Bethel:

Deborah, a prophetess, the wife of Lappidoth, was leading Israel at that time. She held court under the Palm of Deborah between Ramah and Bethel in the hill country of Ephraim, and the Israelites came to her to have their disputes decided (Judges 4:4-5).

In the center of the community is the Arutz 7 radio studio, the voice of the national religious movement in Israel.

Today, Bethel has been rebuilt again. It numbers 1,200 Jewish families.

Samaria
The Biblical Heartland of Israel

The present Samaria includes the old tribal area of the sons of Joseph, Ephraim, and Manasseh. For centuries, this region was considered the center of Israel with Shilo as its capital, where the Holy Ark stood in the Tabernacle. After the reign of King Solomon, Samaria became the heart of the Kingdom of the Ten Tribes which separated from Judah. King Omri built his capital city in Samaria and called it Samaria. Later, the prophet Elijah fought against Ahab in Samaria. The prophets Elisha, Amos, and Hosea also raised their voices here and predicted the coming fall of the northern empire of Israel.

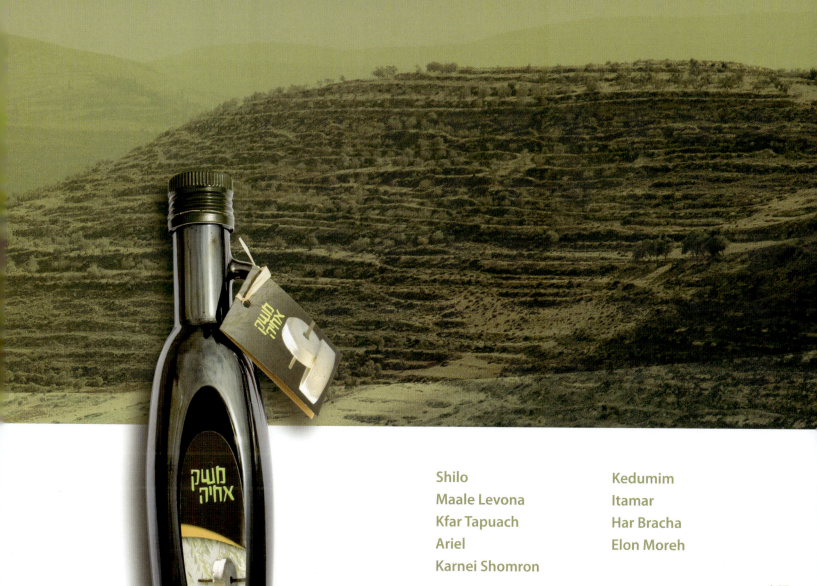

Shilo
Maale Levona
Kfar Tapuach
Ariel
Karnei Shomron

Kedumim
Itamar
Har Bracha
Elon Moreh

In 722 Assyria conquered Samaria, bringing an end to the Kingdom of Israel. During the Second Temple period, the territories of Ephraim and Manasseh were inhabited by the Samaritans, who built a temple of their own on Mount Gerizim. Yet God promised through the mouth of the prophet Ezekiel that in the time of His servant David, the king of the end of days, Ephraim would once again unite with Judah (see Ezek. 37:15-17). The faithfulness of the Lord would overcome the antagonisms within Israel.

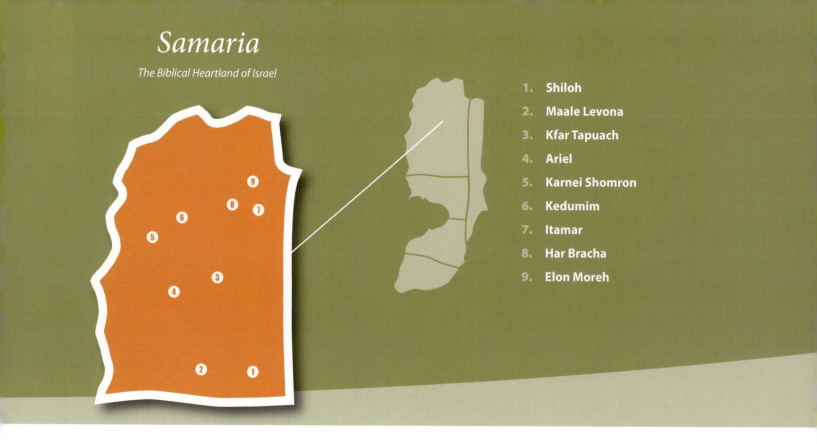

Samaria
The Biblical Heartland of Israel

1. Shiloh
2. Maale Levona
3. Kfar Tapuach
4. Ariel
5. Karnei Shomron
6. Kedumim
7. Itamar
8. Har Bracha
9. Elon Moreh

About Joseph he said: "May the Lord bless his land with the precious dew from heaven above and with the deep waters that lie below; with the best the sun brings forth and the finest the moon can yield; with the choicest gifts of the ancient mountains and the fruitfulness of the everlasting hills; with the best gifts of the earth and its fullness and the favor of Him who dwelt in the burning bush. Let all these rest on the head of Joseph, on the brow of the prince among his brothers" (Deuteronomy 33:13-16).

"Is not Ephraim My dear son, the child in whom I delight? Though I often speak against him, I still remember him. Therefore My heart yearns for him; I have great compassion for him," declares the Lord (Jeremiah 31:20).

Shilo
Samaria, the Biblical Heartland of Israel

During the period of the Judges, Israel assembled in Shilo to worship the Lord. For 369 years, the tabernacle with the Ark of the Covenant stood here.

It was also the sanctuary in which Eli, the high priest, performed his service and Hannah prayed for a son. When the Lord answered her prayer, she called her son Samuel, for she said: "I have asked him of the Lord" (1 Sam. 1:20 NASB).

The modern-day community of Shilo was established in the spring of 1978, together with eleven other modern resettlements of biblical cities such as Bethel and Tekoa. It numbers more than 2,000 residents and its synagogue is built as a replica of the tabernacle.

Shilo has a strong relationship with its neighboring villages, Eli, Maale Levona, and Shevut Rachel, and it is surrounded by the beautiful Shilo Valley with its orchards and olives groves.

Shevut Rachel was founded after the murder of Rachel Druk. The name means "the return of Rachel," and it refers to the famous text of Jeremiah which predicts the return from exile as well as to Rachel whose memory lives on in the village that is named after her.

Shilo was also the residence of the prophet Achiah, the teacher of Elijah, according to the Jewish tradition.

Eli answered, "Go in peace, and may the God of Israel grant you what you have asked of Him." She said, "May your servant find favor in your eyes." Then she went her way and ate something, and her face was no longer downcast (1 Samuel 1:17-18).

This is what the Lord says: "A voice is heard in Ramah, mourning and great weeping, Rachel weeping for her children and refusing to be comforted, because her children are no more." This is what the Lord says: "Restrain your voice from weeping and your eyes from tears, for your work will be rewarded," declares the Lord. "They will return from the land of the enemy. So there is hope for your future," declares the Lord. "Your children will return to their own land" (Jeremiah 31:15-17).

Maale Levona
Samaria, the Biblical Heartland of Israel

Across the road from Shilo—along the Path of the Patriarchs, between Bethel and Shechem—lies Maale Levona (the heights of Levona), a village that was closely related to Shilo in biblical times. Levona is also one of the species that was used for the altar of incense.

Maale Levona was established in 1984 and numbers more than 100 families. Future plans call for an additional 100 homes to be built.

The community is also home to a well-known yeshiva high school for girls where 190 girls are educated in the Chasidic tradition. Maale Levona is an established community where religious Jews from divergent backgrounds have chosen to live together.

The Lord appeared to us in the past, saying: "I have loved you with an everlasting love; I have drawn you with loving-kindness. I will build you up again and you will be rebuilt, O Virgin Israel. Again you will take up your tambourines and go out to dance with the joyful. Again you will plant vineyards on the hills of Samaria; the farmers will plant them and enjoy their fruit. There will be a day when watchmen cry out on the hills of Ephraim, 'Come, let us go up to Zion, to the Lord our God'" (Jeremiah 31:3-6).

Kfar Tapuach
Samaria, the Biblical Heartland of Israel

Tapuach is mentioned in the Book of Joshua as a border city between Ephraim and Manasseh (Josh. 17:8).

Today, there are some 130 families living in Tapuach, with an unusually large number of children. During the past five years, more than 40 young couples joined the community. Many study at the nearby university center of Ariel or work as schoolteachers in Tapuach.

From Tapuach one can see Shechem to the north, spread across the valley between the mountains of Ebal and Gerizim.

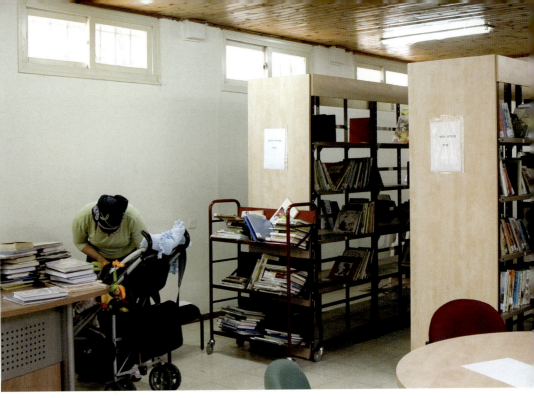

In the kindergarten alone, there are forty children in the three year-old age group.

Christians for Israel supported the furnishing of the new library and the building of a new daycare center for the children.

O Lord, our Lord, how majestic is Your name in all the earth! You have set Your glory above the heavens. From the lips of children and infants You have ordained praise because of Your enemies, to silence the foe and the avenger (Psalm 8:1-2).

Ariel
Samaria, the Biblical Heartland of Israel

Ariel was founded in 1978 and has some 17,000 residents, including a large number of immigrants from the former Soviet Union.

The name of the city refers to Jerusalem. Joshua's tomb is located nearby.

Ariel has a university center, the only one in Judea and Samaria. The well-known Eshel Hashomron Hotel boasts a sculpture garden which depicts the biblical history of Samaria.

Then the hordes of all the nations that fight against Ariel, that attack her and her fortress and besiege her, will be as it is with a dream, with a vision in the night—as when a hungry man dreams that he is eating, but he awakens, and his hunger remains; as when a thirsty man dreams that he is drinking, but he awakens faint, with his thirst unquenched. So will it be with the hordes of all the nations that fight against Mount Zion (Isaiah 29:7-8).

Karnei Shomron
Samaria, the Biblical Heartland of Israel

Northwest of Ariel, not far from Shechem, is Karnei Shomron, a thriving town founded in 1977 with close to 8,000 residents.

In 2002, a terrorist murdered three teenagers in the local shopping center. They were only 15 years old.

There is a plaque on a wall of the shopping center in memory of Rachel, Keren, and Nehemia. On it are inscribed the prophetic words of Zechariah:

And the streets of the city will be filled with boys and girls playing in its streets (Zechariah 8:5 NASB).

These words don't seem to encompass the reality of Israel in the midst of so much enmity. Each step on the road to peace with the Arabs has only evoked more terror, but the Lord adds these words:

This is what the Lord Almighty says: "It may seem marvelous to the remnant of this people at that time, but will it seem marvelous to Me?" declares the Lord Almighty (Zechariah 8:6).

Children are busy baking Matzoth for the coming Passover.

 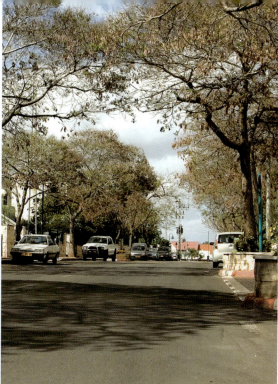 

Karnei Shomron is home to the Israeli headquarters of CFOIC Heartland (Christian Friends of Israeli Communities), the organization which enables Christians to support the Jewish communities of Judea and Samaria and the former residents of Gush Katif.

Kedumim
Samaria, the Biblical Heartland of Israel

The Yom Kippur War of 1973, which the enemies of Israel launched on the holiest day of the year, served as a wake-up call to Jews all over Israel. It was a call from the Lord to His people to settle the desolate and barren land of Samaria and to make it bloom once again.

Kedumim, not far from Shechem and the mountains of Gerizim and Ebal, was the first settlement born of that wake-up call, founded in 1975 after seven unsuccessful attempts.

Many more communities would follow the lead of Kedumim. Today, there are 4,000 people living in Kedumim.

The village is spread across ten hilltops. Har Hemed, where 15 families live in trailers, is the newest hilltop neighborhood.

Kedumim has no fence, but there is a security center where young people, as part of their "national service," operate a sophisticated camera system which closely monitors the entire area.

Kedumin has an excellent high school for girls. One hundred and twenty of the 840 students are new immigrants from Ethiopia. The Lehava High School for Girls is doing wonders for this talented group of immigrants, providing them with a superior education and absorbing them, the remnants of the Tribe of Dan, into Israeli society.

Many young people return to Kedumim to settle as adults after their army service and academic studies.

In that day the Lord will reach out His hand a second time to reclaim the remnant that is left of His people from Assyria, from Lower Egypt, from Upper Egypt, from Cush, from Elam, from Babylonia, from Hamath and from the islands of the sea. He will raise a banner for the nations and gather the exiles of Israel; He will assemble the scattered daughters of Judah from the four quarters of the earth (Isaiah 11:11-12).

Itamar
Samaria, the Biblical Heartland of Israel

Itamar, situated on the mountains east of Shechem, is named after one of the sons of the first high priest of Israel, Aaron.

The community numbers more than 80 families and was hard hit by the terrorism of the second Intifada. A terrorist attack on the Yeshiva, where five boys were murdered, is but one example. Even today, Arabs from the neighboring villages try to infiltrate Itamar with no other goal than to murder Jews.

The Tomb of Joseph is located in Shechem, and the brave inhabitants of Itamar visit this holy place to seek the face of the Lord whenever possible.

After Jacob came from Paddan Aram, he arrived safely at the city of Shechem in Canaan and camped within sight of the city. For a hundred pieces of silver, he bought from the sons of Hamor, the father of Shechem, the plot of ground where he pitched his tent. There he set up an altar and called it El Elohe Israel (Genesis 33:18-20).

And Joseph's bones, which the Israelites had brought up from Egypt, were buried at Shechem in the tract of land that Jacob bought for a hundred pieces of silver from the sons of Hamor, the father of Shechem. This became the inheritance of Joseph's descendants (Joshua 24:32).

Har Bracha
Samaria, the Biblical Heartland of Israel

Har Bracha (the mountain of the blessing) is the name of a Jewish village on Mount Gerizim.

After the entry to the Promised Land, Joshua instructed half of the nation to stand on Mount Ebal and the other half on Mount Gerizim while the blessings and the curses were recited to the people.

In the time of Nehemiah, the Samaritans built a sanctuary on the mountain as a counterpart to the rebuilt temple in Jerusalem. The only remaining community of Samaritans is split today between the Israeli city of Holon and the original community on Mt. Gerizim.

Har Bracha numbers 1,200 inhabitants and has a Hesder Yeshiva, where young men combine their compulsory army service with religious education. The yeshiva students also help with the education of the children in the community and take turns guarding the village. Many of the students make their home in Har Bracha after completing their military service.

All Israel, aliens and citizens alike, with their elders, officials and judges, were standing on both sides of the ark of the covenant of the Lord, facing those who carried it—the priests, who were Levites. Half of the people stood in front of Mount Gerizim and half of them in front of Mount Ebal, as Moses the servant of the Lord had formerly commanded when he gave instructions to bless the people of Israel. Afterward, Joshua read all the words of the law—the blessings and the curses—just as it is written in the Book of the Law. There was not a word of all that Moses had commanded that Joshua did not read to the whole assembly of Israel, including the women and children, and the aliens who lived among them (Joshua 8:33-35).

Elon Moreh
Samaria, the Biblical Heartland of Israel

Elon Moreh was the first stop of Abram in the Promised Land. At the oak tree of Moreh he pitched his tents, and from the top of the mountain he could see the entire country.

This is probably the reason that God did not mention the borders of the land as part of His initial promise to Abram in Elon Moreh.

To the east, Abram could see the mountains of Gilead, in present-day Jordan; to the north he could see in the distance the peaks of the Hermon; in the west lay the coastal plain, and to the south he could see as far as the desert.

Today, Elon Moreh is the modern-day home of 1,200 residents. Like so many other communities in the area, it too has suffered terribly from terrorist attacks. On the Elon Moreh website, one can read the following story, taken from a well-known Jewish source.

A parable is given in Midrash Rabba (Ch. 30):

"A father and son were traveling a long distance together. The son was getting tired and asked his father, 'Where is the city we are headed for?' The father answered, 'My son, you will have a sure sign that a city is near when you see a cemetery.' So the Almighty has said to Israel, 'If you see that your troubles are too much to bear, that is the time when the redemption is near.'"

As it is written in Tehillim 20:

"The L-rd answers you in the day of trouble, the name of the God of Jacob set you up high—Remember your meal-offerings and animal offerings burnt on the altar."

Abram travelled through the land as far as the site of the great tree of Moreh at Shechem. At that time the Canaanites were in the land. The Lord appeared to Abram and said, "To your offspring I will give this land." So he built an altar there to the Lord, who had appeared to him (Genesis 12:6-7).

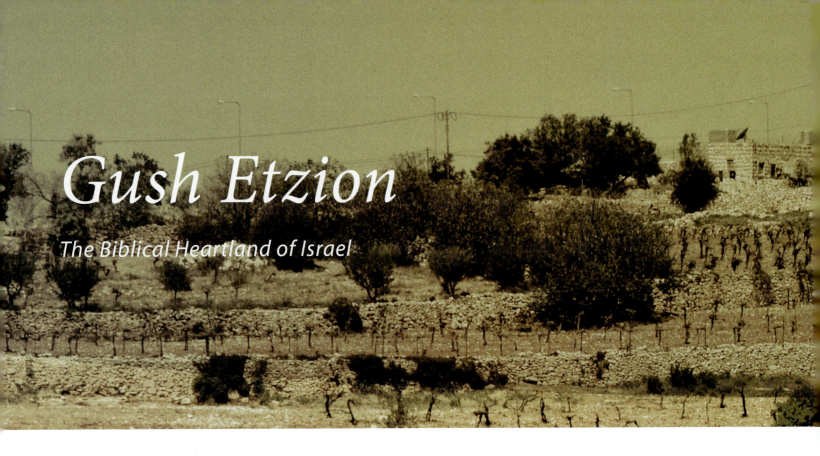

Gush Etzion

The Biblical Heartland of Israel

Gush Etzion is a bloc of Jewish communities which were destroyed by Arabs in May of 1948, the night before the declaration of the State of Israel. Nearly all the male inhabitants of Kfar Etzion, one of the four original communities, sacrificed their lives in a heroic attempt to secure the southern entrance to Jerusalem. Their children returned after the Six Day War and rebuilt the communities that their parents died trying to protect. Gush Etzion will remain a symbol, forever, of the steadfastness of the Jewish people and their dedication to the Land that the Lord promised to Israel.

Kfar Etzion
Bat Ayin
Tekoa
Bethlehem
Efrat

Israel
With the biblical heartland and Gush Kutif

Yesha
The biblical territories Judea, Samaria and Jerusalem

1. Benjamin
2. Samaria
3. Gush Etzion
4. The Mountains of Hebron
5. The Jordan Valley

Jerusalem

Prime Minister David Ben Gurion said in 1948:

"I can think of no battle in the annals of the Israel defense Forces which was more magnificent, more tragic or more heroic than the struggle for Gush Etzion…If there exists a Jewish Jerusalem, our foremost thanks go to the defenders of Gush Etzion."

The region belongs to the tribal area of Judah and is steeped in biblical history.

Gush Etzion

The Biblical Heartland of Israel

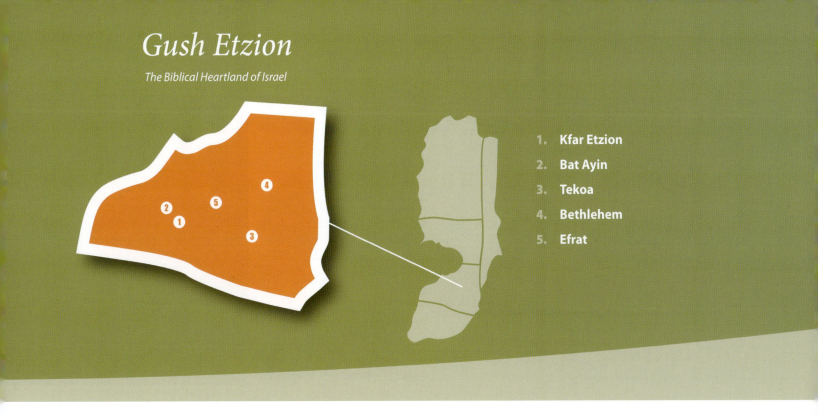

1. Kfar Etzion
2. Bat Ayin
3. Tekoa
4. Bethlehem
5. Efrat

Judah is a lion's whelp; From the prey, my son, you have gone up He couches, he lies down as a lion, And as a lion, who dares rouse him up? The scepter shall not depart from Judah, Nor the ruler's staff from between his feet, Until Shiloh comes, And to him shall be the obedience of the peoples (Genesis 49:9-10 NASB).

Kfar Etzion
Gush Etzion, the Biblical Heartland of Israel

Kfar Etzion is home to 400 residents. In addition to some small industry and agriculture, Kfar Etzion has a museum that is dedicated to the history of the Etzion Bloc. When Kfar Etzion was destroyed in 1947, only one old tree was left standing. All the other trees and buildings were razed to the ground by the Arabs. This lone oak tree could be seen from a distance by the survivors and became the symbol of their determination and their hope to return some day.

They will build houses and dwell in them; they will plant vineyards and eat their fruit. No longer will they build houses and others live in them, or plant and others eat. For as the days of a tree, so will be the days of My people; My chosen ones will long enjoy the works of their hands (Isaiah 65:21-22).

"The days are coming," declares the Lord, "when the reaper will be overtaken by the plowman and the planter by the one treading grapes. New wine will drip from the mountains and flow from all the hills" (Amos 9:13).

The surroundings of Kfar Etzion with their characteristic terraced fields.

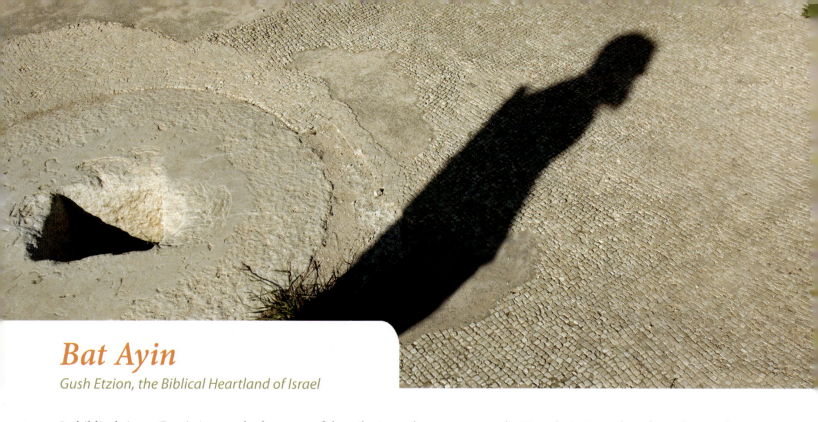

Bat Ayin
Gush Etzion, the Biblical Heartland of Israel

In biblical times, Bat Ayin was the last stop of the pilgrims who went up to the Temple in Jerusalem from the southern areas of Israel. Here we find the wine cellars where the wines of the numerous vineyards were kept in stone vessels. There are also ritual baths, fed by the waters of the natural springs that have given the village the name Bat Ayin (daughter of the springs). From ancient times, Bat Ayin was a place with great spiritual significance. Here the pious prepared themselves for their encounter with God in Zion.

Today, there are 1,000 people living in Bat Ayin, including the students and teachers of the Breslauer Yeshiva under the inspiring leadership of Rabbi Natan Greenberg. For the students, worship, music, and love are central to their dedication to the Lord.

Shout for joy to the Lord, all the earth. Worship the Lord with gladness; come before Him with joyful songs. Know that the Lord is God. It is He who made us, and we are His; we are His people, the sheep of His pasture (Psalm 100:1-3).

My lover has gone down to his garden, to the beds of spices, to browse in the gardens and to gather lilies. I am my lover's and my lover is mine; he browses among the lilies. You are beautiful, my darling, as Tirzah, lovely as Jerusalem, majestic as troops with banners (Song of Solomon 6:2-4).

Tekoa
Gush Etzion, the Biblical Heartland of Israel

The town is known in the Bible from the times of King David, but most of all as the residence of the prophet Amos (see 2 Sam. 14:1-6).

The present Tekoa was established in 1978 and has five neighborhoods covering a number of surrounding hilltops: Tekoa Bet, Gimel, and Dalet (B, C, and D). It numbers 400 families.

Today, Tekoa means life!

After the opening of the new road between Jerusalem and Tekoa and Nokdim, the village bubbles with energy and optimism. New houses are being built and new undertakings have started.

In that day I will restore David's fallen tent. I will repair its broken places, restore its ruins, and build it as it used to be (Amos 9:11).

In 2001, the community was rocked by the murder of two boys, Yosef Ishran and Koby Mandel. While they were collecting wood for a holiday bonfire in the valley just below the village, they were killed in a brutal manner.

Yehuda and Yitzchak in their new olive press. This year they managed to produce 10,000 liters of top-quality oil, a continuation of an old tradition. Once, Tekoa provided the temple of Jerusalem with the purest olive oil. At the Tekoa Mushroom Farm all kinds of mushrooms are cultivated, as well as asparagus and chicory.

The words of Amos, one of the shepherds of Tekoa—what he saw concerning Israel two years before the earthquake, when Uzziah was king of Judah and Jeroboam son of Jehoash was king of Israel (Amos 1:1).

Surely the Sovereign Lord does nothing without revealing His plan to His servants the prophets. The lion has roared—who will not fear? The Sovereign Lord has spoken—who can but prophesy? (Amos 3:7-8)

Bethlehem
Gush Etzion, the Biblical Heartland of Israel

Bethlehem is the city where Naomi and Ruth lived and where David was born. The prophet Micah predicted that in this town the Messiah, the great King of Israel, would appear.

Today, Bethlehem is governed by the Palestinians and it is forbidden for Jews to enter the city!

But you, Bethlehem Ephrathah, though you are small among the clans of Judah, out of you will come one for Me, one who will be ruler over Israel, whose origins are from old, from ancient times (Micah 5:2).

The only place where Jews have free access, although under strong safety measures, is Rachel's tomb (Kever Rachel). Jacob buried her on the way to Efrat, when she had died after she gave birth to her second son, Benjamin.

So Rachel died and was buried on the way to Ephrath (that is, Bethlehem). Over her tomb Jacob set up a pillar, and to this day that pillar marks Rachel's tomb (Genesis 35:19-20).

Efrat
Gush Etzion, the Biblical Heartland of Israel

Not far from Bethlehem lies the new Jewish city Efrat. With more than 7,000 residents, it is the largest community in Gush Etzion.

I will allow no sleep to my eyes, no slumber to my eyelids, till I find a place for the Lord, a dwelling for the Mighty One of Jacob. We heard it in Ephrathah, we came upon it in the fields of Jaar (Psalm 132:5-6).

The southern extension of the Path of the Patriarchs, dating back to the days of Abraham, Isaac, and Jacob, is located near the city of Efrat.

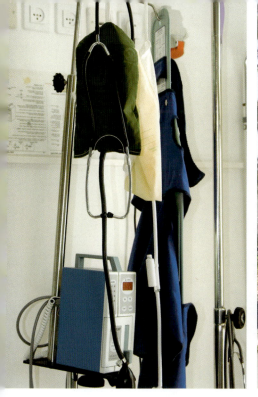

The Efrat Emergency Center is located in the center of the town and played a very important role during the last Intifada. It saved the lives of so many victims of terrorist attacks and provided vital services to residents when the road to Jerusalem was closed.

The Mountains of Hebron
The Biblical Heartland of Israel

To the south of Gush Etzion is the centuries-old city of Hebron. Beyond Hebron, the Judean Hills stretch on toward the Negev. Here the patriarchs pitched their tents and David sojourned before he chose Jerusalem as his capital city.

Hebron
Maon
Sussya
Beit Yatir
Otniel
Shani Livneh

Israel
With the biblical heartland and Gush Kutif

Yesha
The biblical territories Judea, Samaria and Jerusalem

1. Benjamin
2. Samaria
3. Gush Etzion
4. The Mountains of Hebron
5. The Jordan Valley

Jerusalem

The eternal God is your refuge, and underneath are the everlasting arms.
He will drive out your enemies before you, saying, "Destroy them!"
So Israel will live in safety; Jacob will dwell secure in a land of grain and new wine, where the heavens drop dew.
Blessed are you, Israel!

The Mountains of Hebron

The Biblical Heartland of Israel

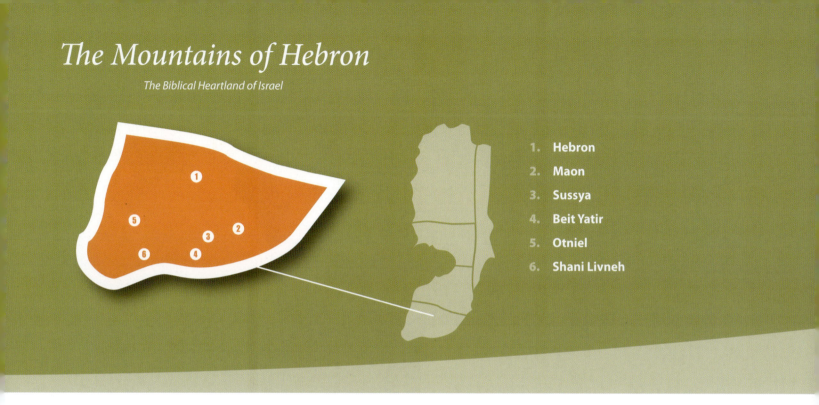

1. Hebron
2. Maon
3. Sussya
4. Beit Yatir
5. Otniel
6. Shani Livneh

Who is like you, a people saved by the Lord?
He is your shield and helper and your glorious sword. Your enemies will cower before you, and you will tread on their heights (Deuteronomy 33:27-29).

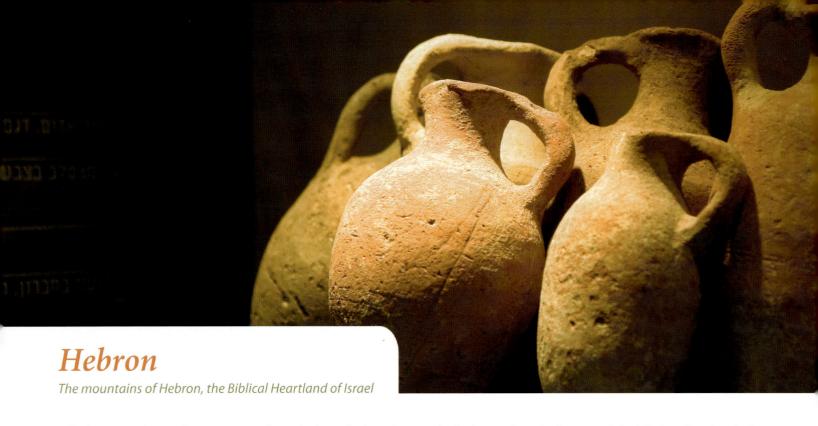

Hebron

The mountains of Hebron, the Biblical Heartland of Israel

Abraham agreed to Ephron's terms and weighed out for him the price he had named in the hearing of the Hittites: four hundred shekels of silver, according to the weight current among the merchants. So Ephron's field in Machpelah near Mamre—both the field and the cave in it, and all the trees within the borders of the field—was deeded to Abraham as his property in the presence of all the Hittites who had come to the gate of the city. Afterward Abraham buried his wife Sarah in the cave in the field of Machpelah near Mamre (which is at Hebron) in the land of Canaan (Genesis 23:16-19).

In Hebron we find the cave of Machpela, where the patriarchs and matriarchs are buried. Later, the town became King David's capital city during the first seven years of his rein.

After the death of Saul and his sons, David asked the Lord where he should reside:

In the course of time, David inquired of the Lord. "Shall I go up to one of the towns of Judah?" he asked. The Lord said, "Go up." David asked, "Where shall I go?" "To Hebron," the Lord answered. …Then the men of Judah came to Hebron and there they anointed David king over the house of Judah… (2 Samuel 2:1,4).

Modern Hebron is well-known for the Arab massacre of the local Jews in 1929.

In 1968, Jews returned to Hebron and the old Jewish quarter was brought to life once more. The centuries-old synagogue, which was destroyed by the Arabs and the site used as a public toilet, was uncovered and restored as the central synagogue of the community. Today, there are 800 Jews living in Hebron itself—brave men, women, and children who live a hard life surrounded by tens of thousands of Arabs.

The adjacent Kiryat Arba has a Jewish population of 8,000. Central to the community is the Museum of Judah which teaches the youth of Israel the biblical and ancient history of the region.

Maon
The mountains of Hebron, the Biblical Heartland of Israel

A certain man in Maon, who had property there at Carmel, was very wealthy. He had a thousand goats and three thousand sheep, which he was shearing in Carmel (1 Samuel 25:2).

When David asks Nabal for a gift—because he has always treated him with respect and has also protected his flocks—Nabal refuses bluntly and replies to David's men:

…Who is this David? Who is this son of Jesse? Many servants are breaking away from their masters these days. Why should I take my bread and water, and the meat I have slaughtered for my shearers, and give it to men coming from who knows where? (1 Samuel 25:10-11)

When David reacts indignantly and marches out to punish the foolish Nabal, the wife of Nabal, Abigail, goes to meet David with bread, wine, and sheep meat, greeting him with these words:

Please forgive your servant's offence, for the Lord will certainly make a lasting dynasty for my master, because he fights the Lord's battles. Let no wrongdoing be found in you as long as you live (1 Samuel 25:28).

The story ends when the Lord slays Nabal and David asks the wise Abigail to become his wife.

There are two Jewish villages south of Hebron named Maon and Carmel.

Sussya
The mountains of Hebron, the Biblical Heartland of Israel

Sussya, in the territory of Caleb, was founded in 1984 and today has a population of 120 families, including 500 children. The community has a Yeshiva High School, where students combine lessons in Bible and Talmud with environmental studies.

In Sussya there is a prayer house that is a replica of the old synagogue.

Outside the modern village we find the ruins of the second-century Sussya that once counted more than 6,000 inhabitants.

They will rebuild the ancient ruins and restore the places long devastated; they will renew the ruined cities that have been devastated for generations (Isaiah 61:4).

Beit Yatir
The mountains of Hebron, the Biblical Heartland of Israel

On the edge of the desert, at a height of 900 meters, lies Beit Yatir, a religious orthodox community of 75 families. The village was established in 1983 and is inhabited by Jews that have made aliyah ("returned to the land") from France, Brazil, Russia, and the United States.

In biblical times, Yatir was one of the 48 Levite cities (see Josh. 21:14).

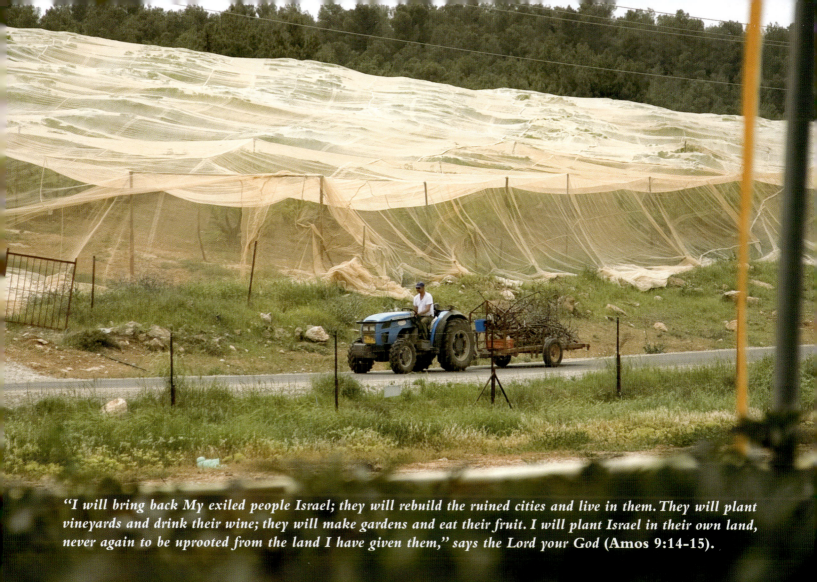

"I will bring back My exiled people Israel; they will rebuild the ruined cities and live in them. They will plant vineyards and drink their wine; they will make gardens and eat their fruit. I will plant Israel in their own land, never again to be uprooted from the land I have given them," says the Lord your God (**Amos 9:14-15**).

Beit Yatir lives from what the Promised Land is producing.

Cherries, nectarines, grapes, apples, and peonies are grown here. In addition, Beit Yatir produces one of the best wines of Israel.

Do not be afraid, Jacob, my servant, Jeshurun, whom I have chosen. For I will pour water on the thirsty land, and streams on the dry ground; I will pour out my Spirit on your offspring, and my blessing on your descendants (Isaiah 44:2-3).

Otniel
The mountains of Hebron, the Biblical Heartland of Israel

The community of Otniel was founded in 1983 in the territory of Caleb, and today it is home to 580 people.

But when they cried out to the Lord, He raised up for them a deliverer, Othniel son of Kenaz, Caleb's younger brother, who saved them. The Spirit of the Lord came upon him, so that he became Israel's judge and went to war… (Judges 3:9-10).

The Hesder Yeshiva attracts students from all over Israel, owing in part to its success in connecting the Bible and Talmud to modern, everyday life. There are 350 students currently studying in the Yeshiva, and the Bet Midrash (study hall) not only contains countless books, but also computers and a small flyer which says:

"When you can, turn your learning into prayer"—so typical of the message of this Yeshiva.

On the wall of the Yeshiva entrance way is a plaque with the names of the ten victims of Arab terror. On one occasion, in 2002, while students were eating their Sabbath meal in the dining room, terrorists forced their way into the kitchen. One of the students sacrificed his own life by blocking the door to the dining room. Five students were killed that evening in the kitchen, but the lives of the students in the dining room were spared.

Though I constantly take my life in my hands, I will not forget Your law. The wicked have set a snare for me, but I have not strayed from Your precepts. Your statutes are my heritage for ever; they are the joy of my heart. My heart is set on keeping Your decrees to the very end (Psalm 119:109–112).

Shani Livneh
The mountains of Hebron, the Biblical Heartland of Israel

In biblical times, Shani Livneh was a city of refuge. When somebody killed someone by accident, he could run to Shani Livneh and find refuge from a vengeful relative.

Outside the city lie the remains of what was a town of 7,000 inhabitants, Anim (see Josh. 15:50).

Today, Shani Livneh is a community with 105 families, both religious and secular.

The security fence that separates Shani Livneh from the mountains of Hebron has created a new situation. Overnight, the community has become a border town. Initially, this scared off some of the residents who left the community because of increased terrorism in the area. Fortunately, in recent months new and especially young families have come to live in the community and a lot of attention is being paid to new projects that will make Shani Livneh even more attractive to new families. One of them is a new archeological project for teenagers in the old Anim.

It is a miracle to see how the village with her forests, fruit trees, and vineyards flourishes in the heat of the desert.

And Jacob blessed his son Judah:

He will tether his donkey to a vine, his colt to the choicest branch; he will wash his garments in wine, his robes in the blood of grapes. His eyes will be darker than wine, his teeth whiter than milk (Genesis 49:11-12).

This is what the Lord says—He who made you, who formed you in the womb, and who will help you: Do not be afraid, O Jacob, My servant, Jeshurun, whom I have chosen. For I will pour water on the thirsty land, and streams on the dry ground; I will pour out My Spirit on your offspring, and My blessing on your descendants (Isaiah 44:2-3).

The Jordan Valley

The Biblical Heartland of Israel

The Jordan Valley stretches from Jericho in the south until Beth Shean in the north. From 1948 until 1967, the area was occupied by Jordan and was considered a military zone. After the Six Day War, the region fell to Israel, which developed it into an important agricultural area. The more than 6,000 people who brought the dry and arid valley to prosperity are spread across 26 communities.

Gilgal
Maale Efraim
Fazael
Hemdath
Maskiot
Shadmot Mechola

After the arrival of the Israelis, Arabs began to live in the area as well, starting their own agricultural enterprises and making use of Jewish knowledge and expertise.

The 80 kilometer long strip has important strategic value because it forms Israel's eastern border with Jordan. On both sides of the Jordan River one can see, as far as the eye reaches, numerous greenhouses and date groves. The area that lies at the foot of the mountains of Samaria belongs to the tribal territory of Ephraim and Manasseh.

The Jordan Valley
The Biblical Heartland of Israel

1. Gilgal
2. Maale Ephraim
3. Fazael
4. Hemdat
5. Maskiot
6. Shadmot Mechola

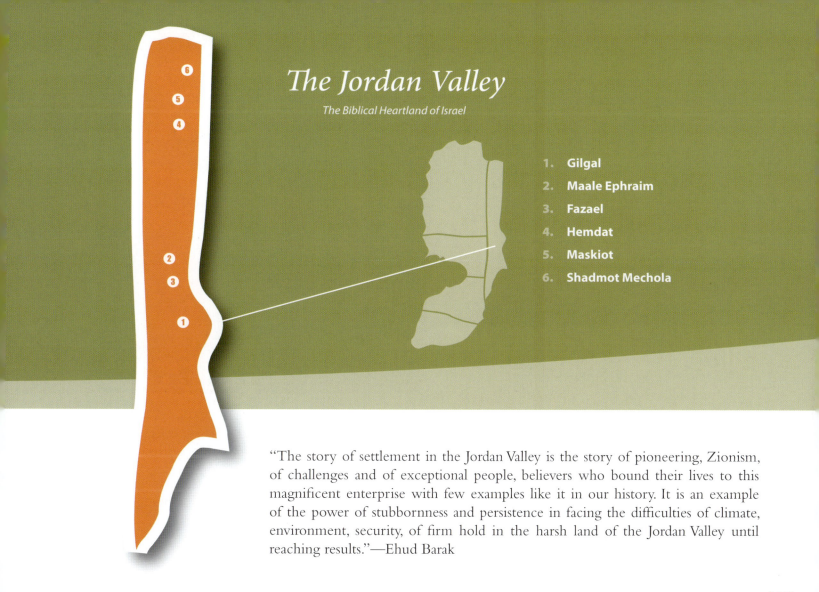

"The story of settlement in the Jordan Valley is the story of pioneering, Zionism, of challenges and of exceptional people, believers who bound their lives to this magnificent enterprise with few examples like it in our history. It is an example of the power of stubbornness and persistence in facing the difficulties of climate, environment, security, of firm hold in the harsh land of the Jordan Valley until reaching results."—Ehud Barak

Gilgal
The Jordan Valley, the Biblical Heartland of Israel

Gilgal is where the Jewish people, under the leadership of Joshua, entered Canaan. Here the nation celebrated Passover for the first time in the Promised Land. The day after Passover, they ate the unleavened bread from the produce of the land and the Lord no longer provided mannah from Heaven.

During the period of the Judges and the Kings of Israel, Gilgal remained a prominent city.

Today, Gilgal is a beautiful village in the Jordan Valley with rich date orchards. There are 45 families living in Gilgal.

Fertilization of the date trees is a complicated process.

And Joshua set up at Gilgal the twelve stones they had taken out of the Jordan. He said to the Israelites, "In the future when your descendants ask their fathers, 'What do these stones mean?' tell them, 'Israel crossed the Jordan on dry ground.' For the Lord your God dried up the Jordan before you until you had crossed over. The Lord your God did to the Jordan just what He had done to the Red Sea when He dried it up before us until we had crossed over. He did this so that all the peoples of the earth might know that the hand of the Lord is powerful and so that you might always fear the Lord your God" (Joshua 4:20-24).

Maale Ephraim
The Jordan Valley, the Biblical Heartland of Israel

In the middle of the valley, partly up the mountain, lies the town Maale Ephraim.

It has 1,400 residents and a high school where many young people from the Jordan Valley receive their education.

I will increase the number of men and animals upon you, and they will be fruitful and become numerous. I will settle people on you as in the past and will make you prosper more than before. Then you will know that I am the Lord (Ezekiel 36:11).

  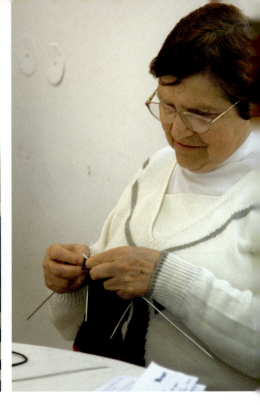

I will cause people, My people Israel, to walk upon you. They will possess you, and you will be their inheritance; you will never again deprive them of their children (Ezekiel 36:12).

You will go out in joy and be led forth in peace; the mountains and hills will burst into song before you, and all the trees of the field will clap their hands. Instead of the thornbush will grow the pine tree, and instead of briers the myrtle will grow. This will be for the Lord's renown, for an everlasting sign, which will not be destroyed (Isaiah 55:12–13).

Fazael
The Jordan Valley, the Biblical Heartland of Israel

In the heart of the valley lies Fazael, established in 1970 and home to more than 70 families.

Not far from Fazael is a high mountain peak, the Sartaba, where bonfires were lit in biblical and talmudic times to announce the appearance of the new moon. The beacon light seen from the top of the Sartaba was one of a series of such lights used by the Jews of Jerusalem to communicate with the Jewish community of Babylon.

The desert and the parched land will be glad; the wilderness will rejoice and blossom. Like the crocus, it will burst into bloom; it will rejoice greatly and shout for joy. The glory of Lebanon will be given to it, the splendor of Carmel and Sharon; they will see the glory of the Lord, the splendor of our God (Isaiah 35:1–2).

Hemdat
The Jordan Valley, the Biblical Heartland of Israel

Hemdat lies in the north, in the foothills of the Samarian mountains. The hilltop was first used as an observation post of the Israeli army, but when the army no longer had need of this post, students of the pre-military academy of Eli moved there. In 1997, these pioneering students laid the foundation for a new community and founded their own school where young people prepare for their military service by studying the Bible and engaging in intensive physical training.

There are 30 young families living in Hemdat.

Hemdat overlooks the Jordan Valley with a view toward the mountains of Jordan, where the Yabbok river empties into the Jordan.

That night Jacob got up and took his two wives, his two maidservants and his eleven sons and crossed the ford of the Jabbok. After he had sent them across the stream, he sent over all his possessions. So Jacob was left alone, and a man wrestled with him till daybreak (Genesis 32:22-24).

Maskiot

The Jordan Valley, the Biblical Heartland of Israel

In August of 2005, the people of Gush Katif were expelled from their villages and their houses were destroyed.

A number of families from Shirat Hayam finally found a new future in Maskiot, on the site of a former army camp.

Here, they work hard to make new lives for themselves as they try to build a new community. Olive trees have been planted and date palms are being tended before final planting.

There are eight families living in Maskiot.

The community leader is the energetic Yossi Chazut.

He is guided in his work by Psalm 127:1:

Unless the Lord builds the house, its builders labor in vain. Unless the Lord watches over the city, the watchmen stand guard in vain.

Shadmot Mechola
The Jordan Valley, the Biblical Heartland of Israel

Shadmot Mechola began 25 years ago on the site of current-day Maskiot. Since then, the community has grown into an oasis in the desert valley. There are 600 people living in Shadmot Mechola today, with an additional 200 young men who study in the local Hesder Yeshiva, which combines a religious education with military service.

Together with Mechola and Roi, Shadmot Mechola is an important agricultural area.

From the observation point, one has a magnificent view of the mountains of Gilboa, the valley itself, and the eastern bank of the Jordan—biblical Gilead, where the prophet Elijah was born. Here, too, is where Yabesh was situated, the town that was saved by King Saul and that showed her gratitude by removing the corpses of Saul and his sons which the Philistines hung on the city walls of Beth Shean, and by giving them an honorable burial in their own town.

The army has cleared the minefields between Shadmot Medchola and the Jordan River and paved the way for the planting of new crops. In the eyes of the people of the village, it is a modern fulfillment of the words of the prophet Isaiah:

They will beat their swords into ploughshares and their spears into pruning hooks… (Isaiah 2:4).

Abel Mechola was the residence of the prophet Elisha (see 1 Kings 19:16).

So Elijah went from there and found Elisha son of Shaphat. He was plowing with twelve yoke of oxen, and he himself was driving the twelfth pair. Elijah went up to him and threw his cloak around him. Elisha then left his oxen and ran after Elijah. "Let me kiss my father and mother good-bye," he said, "and then I will come with you." "Go back," Elijah replied. "What have I done to you?" So Elisha left him and went back. He took his yoke of oxen and slaughtered them. He burned the plowing equipment to cook the meat and gave it to the people, and they ate. Then he set out to follow Elijah and became his attendant (1 Kings 19:19-21).

*They will say, "This land that was laid waste has become like the garden of Eden;
the cities that were lying in ruins, desolate and destroyed, are now fortified and inhabited."*

Then the nations around you that remain will know that I the Lord have rebuilt what was destroyed and have replanted what was desolate.

I the Lord have spoken, and I will do it (Ezekiel 36:35-36).

On that day living water will flow out from Jerusalem, half to the eastern sea and half to the western sea, in summer and in winter (Zechariah 14:8).

About the Author

Rev. Henk Poot was born in the Netherlands in 1955 and is an ordained pastor of the Protestant Church of the Netherlands. He currently works full time for Christians for Israel, Holland. He speaks and writes on the subject of the Church and Israel in Holland and Europe. He is also director of CFOIC Heartland in the Netherlands. He is the author of five books, including *Christian Paganism* (2003) and *Daniel, the Visions* (2007). Fluent in English and German as well as his native Dutch, Rev. Poot resides in the Netherlands with his wife and nine children.

About the Photographer and Graphic Designer

Theo Horneman, a freelance graphic designer and photographer, was born in Holland in 1966. He made his first trip to Israel in 2005 but was imbued with the love of Israel from a very young age. On that first trip, he met a family from the Samarian community of Neve Zuf with the same last name as his, a connection that turned into a solid friendship. What began as an initial encounter with one community in Samaria became a journey into the meaning and reality that is Judea and Samaria, a journey that has culminated with this photographic essay. Theo lives in the Netherlands with his wife and three children.

http://www.horneman.net

About C4I and CFOIC Heartland

Christians for Israel is an international, non-denominational movement of Christians who believe that God is faithful to His eternal covenants with the Jewish people. Our mission is to encourage biblical understanding in the Church and among the nations concerning God's purposes for Israel and to promote comfort of Israel through prayer and action.

http://www.c4israel.org
http://www.whyisrael.org

CFOIC Heartland connects Christians from all over the world with the Jewish communities in Judea and Samaria and with the Jewish refugees from Gaza.

http://www.cfoic.com

Proceeds from the sale of this book will be used to support the people of Judea and Samaria.
For more information see http://www.judeaandsamaria.com

Additional copies of this book and other book titles from DESTINY IMAGE™ EUROPE are available at your local bookstore.

We are adding new titles every month!

To view our complete catalog online, visit us at: **www.eurodestinyimage.com**

Send a request for a catalog to:

Via della Scafa 29/14
65013 Città Sant'Angelo (Pe) — Italy
Tel. +39 085 4716623 • +39 085 8670146
info@eurodestinyimage.com

"Changing the world, one book at a time."

Are you an author?
Do you have a "today" God-given message?

CONTACT US

We will be happy to review your manuscript for the possibility of publication:

publisher@eurodestinyimage.com
http://www.eurodestinyimage.com/pages/AuthorsAppForm.htm

Restaurants

Adom ✪✪✪
31 Jaffa St. (Down a side alley). Yuppie atmosphere, an audacious menu and a spacious, red-lit dining area is the charm of Adom, which means red in Hebrew.

Burger's Bar ✪
Shamai St. and Emek Refaim. Noisy and daunting to first timers, this fast-paced order-at-the-counter eatery serves great burgers with a variety of inventive sauces.

Cacao (Cinematek) ✪✪
11 Hebron Rd. An artsy moviegoing crowd frequents this restaurant with dynamic views of the Hinnom Valley and the Old City walls.

Café Rimon ✪✪
4 Lunts Moshe St. (off Ben Yehuda). Meat and dairy dining rooms are separate at this popular downtown eatery.

Caffit ✪✪
37 Emek Refaim. A German Colony favorite serving the standard Israeli restaurant fare from sandwiches to pizzas and pastas.

Focaccia ✪✪
4 Rabbi Akiva St. Great bargains and wide variety from Israeli-style focaccia to pizza, pasta, sandwiches and burgers.

La Rotisserie ✪✪✪
Across from New Gate at the Notre Dame complex. Gourmet French menu and an international crowd frequent this French and very expensive restaurant.

Nafoura ✪✪
18 Latin Patriachate Road, Old (1st street to left inside Jaffa Gate). Classic Middle Eastern cuisine in a beautiful courtyard setting next to the Old City walls.

Paradiso ✪✪✪
36 Keren Hayesod. From the steak sandwich to the hot chocolate cake, every item on the menu is worthy of note.

Rivlin ✪✪
7 Yosef Rivlin St. Elegant outdoor and indoor seating near the pedestrian walkways downtown.

The Ticho House ✪✪
9 HaRav Kook St. Eclectic menu amid a tranquil garden. Jerusalem artichoke and special blintzes are among the daring choices. The indoor of the restaurant is a library.

Vaqueiro ✪✪✪
54 HaNevi'im (Prophets) St. Mix of South American/South African cuisine. Great business lunch offers and all-you-can-eat specials. Highly recommended.

Price guide:
✪ Inexpensive = 20 to 40 NIS
✪✪ Moderate = 40 to 60 NIS
✪✪✪ Expensive = 60 NIS and up